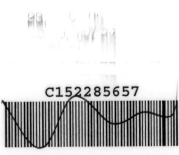

Islands

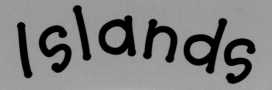

Christopher Durbin

HODDER
Wayland

an imprint of Hodder Children's Books

Geography First

Titles in this series
Coasts • Islands • Maps and Symbols
Mountains • Rivers • Volcanoes

© 2004 White-Thomson Publishing Ltd

Produced for Hodder Wayland by
White-Thomson Publishing Ltd
2/3 St Andrew's Place
Lewes, East Sussex
BN7 1UP

Geography consultant: John Lace, School Adviser
Editor: Katie Orchard
Picture research: Glass Onion Pictures
Designer: Chris Halls at Mind's Eye Design Ltd, Lewes
Artist: Peter Bull

Published in Great Britain in 2004 by Hodder Wayland,
an imprint of Hodder Children's Books.

The right of Christopher Durbin to be identified as the
author has been asserted by him in accordance with
the Copyright, Designs and Patents Act, 1988.

British Library Cataloguing in Publication Data
Durbin, Christopher
  Islands. - (Geography first)
  1. Islands - Juvenile literature
  I. Title II. Orchard, Katie
  551.4'2
ISBN 0 7502 4354 6

Printed in China

Hodder Children's Books
A division of Hodder Headline Limited
338 Euston Road, London NW1 3BH

Cover: The island of Coral Cay, Australia.
Title page: The tropical islands of the Bahamas.
Contents page: Dense rainforest on St Lucia.
Further information page: The Danish island of Stryno
Kalv has only three farmhouses on it.

Acknowledgements:
The author and publisher would like to thank the following for their permission to reproduce the following
photographs: Corbis 9 (Jay Dickman), 16 (Michael S. Lewis), 22 (Bojan Brecelj), 26 (Alan Schein Photography);
Ecoscene 21 (Edward Bent), 24 (Stephen Coyne), 25 (Nick Hanna), 27 (PT); Hodder Wayland Picture Library
title page, chapter openers, 18, 31; NHPA cover; Natural Science Photos 17 (C. Dani and I. Jeske), 19
(I.Bennett); Oxford Scientific Films 5 (Kathie Atkinson), 7 (Ian West), 12 (Norbert Wu), 20 (Robin Bush);
Popperfoto 11 (Reuters/Japan Coast Guard); Still Pictures 4 (Roger de la Harpe), 15 (Gerard and Margi Moss),
23 (Massimo Lupidi); Travel Ink 14 (Geraint Tellem), 28 (Patrick Ford).

Words in bold **like this** are explained in the glossary on page 30.

Contents

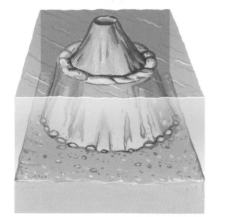

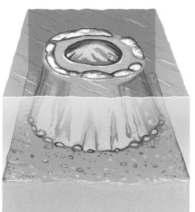

What is an island?

An island is a piece of land surrounded by water. An island is smaller than a **continent** and larger than a rock. Most islands are found in oceans and seas, but some are found in lakes and rivers.

▼ Tiny rocky islands jut out of the sea around Pemba Island, off the coast of Tanzania.

There are many different types of island. Some have hard, rocky **coasts** and others have soft, sandy beaches.

Some islands, like Greenland, are very large. Others are very small and may have little **fresh water**. They are usually **uninhabited**, which means that no one lives on them.

▼ *Masthead Island is part of Australia's Great Barrier Reef. It is very small and has very little fresh water so no one lives on it.*

Rocky islands

Some small, rocky islands are found just off the coast of a large piece of land, or **mainland**. They are usually made of very hard rock.

Over time, the sea **erodes**, or wears away, the softer rock on the mainland. A piece of hard rock may be left behind, forming an island.

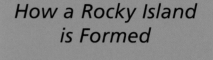

How a Rocky Island is Formed

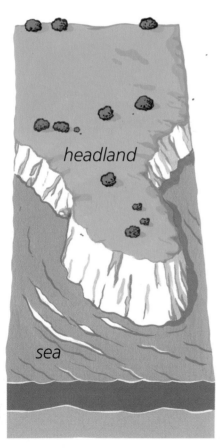

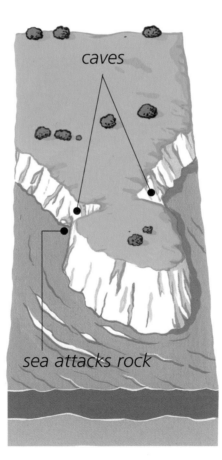

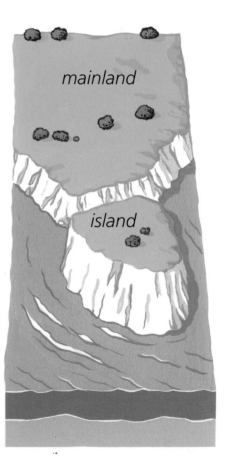

A headland with soft and hard rock areas.

Sea erodes soft rock and wears it away from both sides.

Sea breaks through, leaving a hard rock island and the mainland.

Some rocky islands can be reached at low **tide** when the sea goes out. The low-lying land between the island and the mainland is called a **causeway**. When the tide comes back in, the sea floods the causeway and separates the island from the mainland once more.

▼ *St Michael's Mount in Cornwall, England. When the tide goes out, the causeway is revealed.*

Sand islands

Some islands are made of sand. They form in areas where the sea is shallow. Where the sea **currents** are not very strong, sand builds up slowly to form a **sandbank**. When the tide goes out, sandbanks can be seen as small sandy mounds.

From Sandbank
to Island

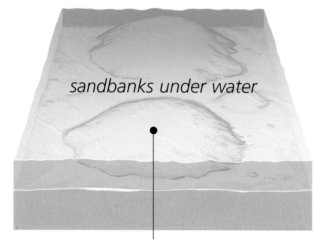

sandbanks under water

Sandbanks develop on seabed.

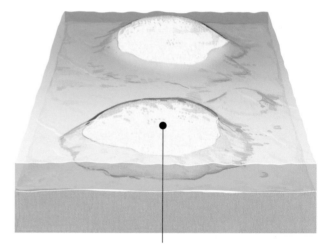

Tide goes out and sandbanks are revealed. Wind blows more sand on to the shore and sandbanks grow.

Sandbanks now remain above sea level even when the tide is in. The sandbanks are now islands.

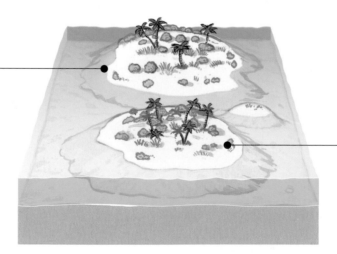

Plants start to grow and sand is trapped, making the islands taller.

Wind blows sand on to the shore. This new sand makes the sandbanks even higher. When the tide comes in, a sandbank may remain out of the water, forming a sandy island. Grass grows on the island and traps more sand, which helps the island grow bigger.

▼ *A fishing boat sails round the Florida Keys, a group of sand islands in the USA.*

Volcanic islands

Some islands are formed by underwater **volcanoes**. Under the Earth's surface is a layer of hot, liquid rock, called **magma**. When magma breaks through the Earth's surface, or **erupts**, a volcano is formed.

Formation of a Volcanic Island

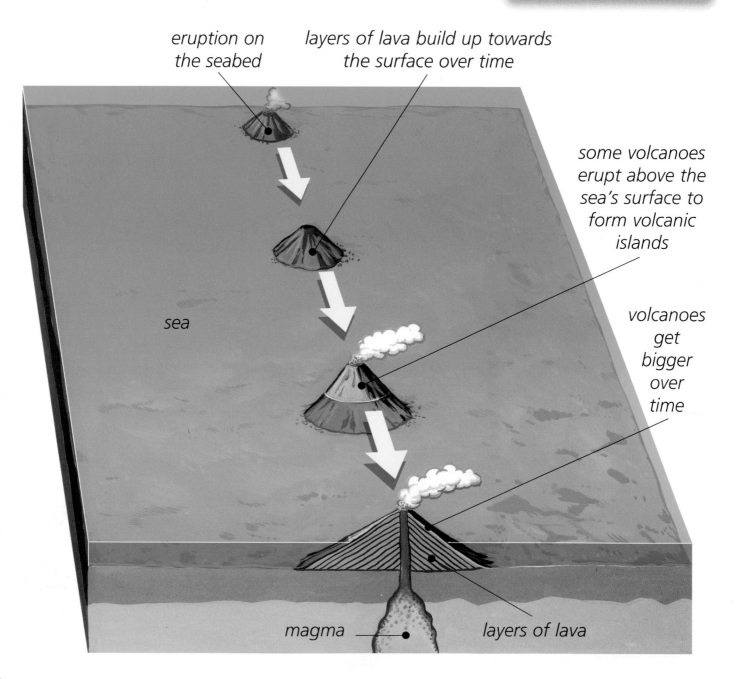

eruption on the seabed

layers of lava build up towards the surface over time

some volcanoes erupt above the sea's surface to form volcanic islands

sea

volcanoes get bigger over time

magma

layers of lava

When magma erupts it is called **lava**. Under the sea, the hot lava cools down quickly to form a layer of solid rock.

Each time the volcano erupts, layers of lava gradually build up on top of one another. In this way the volcano grows. Over time it breaks through the surface of the sea to form an island.

▼ *Smoke billows from the volcanic island of Torishima, in Japan.*

Coral reef islands

Most **coral reefs** are made by small animals that live only in warm, shallow seas. These animals live near to the coast of an island.

▼ *A diver explores a colourful coral reef in the Solomon Islands.*

When the animals grow they leave behind **coral**, which is hard, like rock. Corals grow upwards towards the sea surface.

Many coral reefs form rings around volcanic islands. Over time, the volcano may sink or collapse. The coral island is left behind, with a **lagoon**, or pool, in the middle. This type of island is called an **atoll**.

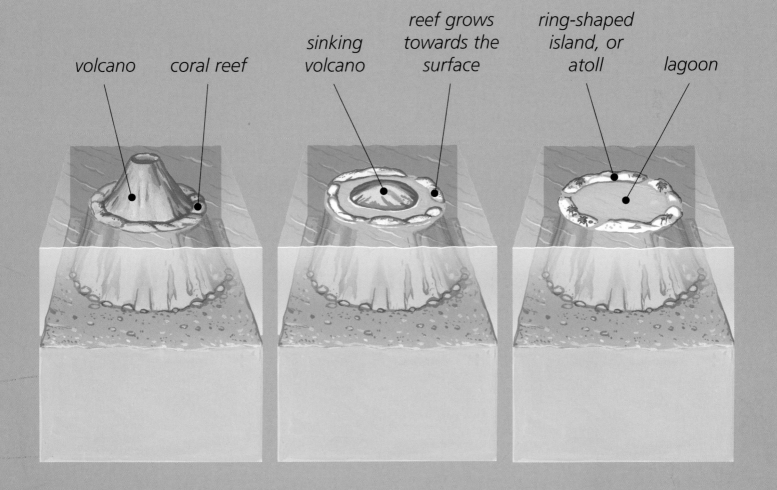

volcano   coral reef   sinking volcano   reef grows towards the surface   ring-shaped island, or atoll   lagoon

A coral reef grows up in the warm, shallow water around a volcanic island.

The volcano sinks and the coral reef continues to grow.

The volcano disappears from sight, leaving the coral reef behind.

Patterns of islands

Islands can form in groups, or patterns. The most common pattern is a curved line of islands, called an **arc**. Usually, an island arc is a line of undersea volcanoes. Over time, the volcanoes erupt along a crack or weakness in the surface of the Earth and grow above sea level.

▼ Oahu is one of many Hawaiian islands that make up an island arc, formed from undersea volcanoes.

An **archipelago** is a group of small islands close together. They are usually found near coasts where the rocks are harder in some places than in others. The sea erodes the softer rock, leaving behind a group of hard rock islands.

▼ *These islands form part of the Juan Fernandez archipelago, which is near Chile.*

Climates and sea levels

Islands do not all have the same **climates**, or weather conditions. How hot or cold an island is depends on where it is in the world. Islands near the **Equator** are very warm and those near the **North Pole** and **South Pole** may be covered with snow and ice all year.

▼ *Snow and ice cover this part of Greenland all year round.*

Sea levels rise and fall over many years. When the sea level falls, more of the sea bed around an island can be seen, and the island may become bigger. When the sea rises, islands may become flooded. Low-lying islands may disappear altogether.

▲ *As sea levels rise, some of these islands in French Polynesia may become smaller, or even disappear.*

Island plants

The plants growing on an island depend on its climate. On **Arctic** islands it is too cold for any trees to grow. Hot, dry, **desert** islands may have very few plants growing on them. Some wet and warm islands are completely covered with dense forest.

▼ *Dense rainforest plants and trees grow on the island of St Lucia.*

At first, new islands have no plants growing on them. The wind blows seeds on to an island from the mainland.

Grasses are usually the first plants to grow. Birds may fly in, bringing seeds in their droppings. Bushes and other plants will then grow from these seeds.

▼ *This Australian sandbank is only revealed at low tide. It does not yet have any plants growing on it.*

Island animals

Many islands are home to animals that are not found anywhere else. This is because they are **isolated**, or separate, from the mainland. Over time the animals that live there have had to **adapt**, or change, to cope with conditions on the island.

▼ *The Kakapo is a rare flightless bird that lives on Stewart Island, New Zealand.*

Some islands used to have flightless birds and no **predators**. When people from Europe explored these islands hundreds of years ago, they brought with them cats and rats. The predators killed off many of the birds, which could not fly away.

▼ A marine iguana comes face to face with two booby birds on the Galapagos Islands. Iguanas are not found anywhere else in the world.

People and islands

Many people live and work on islands. For most islanders, living on an island is the same as living anywhere else.

On some **remote** islands, it is expensive to transport goods and food from other countries. The land may have to be carefully farmed to grow food for the people on the island.

▲ *These men are loading a sailing boat in Zanzibar with cargo. The boat takes goods from the mainland to islands in the Indian Ocean.*

On many small islands, fishing is an important industry. Much of the fish caught is sold to islanders, or to restaurants and supermarkets. The rest is sold to other countries.

▼ Fishermen sort through their catch on the coast of Iceland. Iceland is the third-largest fishing nation in Europe.

Holiday islands

Many people from places with cool or wet climates visit warm islands for a holiday. Tourists enjoy the sun, sea and beautiful scenery. Millions of people from Northern Europe fly to islands in the Mediterranean Sea. People from North America often choose the Caribbean islands.

▼ Thousands of tourists visit the tropical island of Sri Lanka each year. These visitors have come to see baby elephants at the elephant orphanage.

If these islands become too popular, they can become overcrowded. Some islands may run out of fresh water. Litter and building work can damage the beautiful **environment** people have come to see.

▲ *High-rise hotels line Waikiki Beach, in Hawaii. Tourists go there for the white sandy beaches and warm sea.*

Big city islands

Some rivers have islands where they meet the sea. In the past, these were good places for people to settle. People living there could travel to and from faraway places. Some of these islands became **ports**. People came to buy and sell goods and big cities grew.

> ▼ *Manhattan Island is the city centre of New York. Over 1 million people live there.*

When cities grow on islands, they run out of land for building, so the buildings are often very tall.

In some places large amounts of earth and rocks are pushed into the sea to make new flat land to build on. This is called reclaimed land.

▼ *Hong Kong has 7,394,000 people living on 1,092 km². Many of its buildings stand on land reclaimed from the sea.*

Island fact file

1. The largest island in the world is Greenland, at over 2 million km². It is mainly made up mountains covered with snow and ice.

2. The second-largest island is New Guinea.

3. Java, Indonesia (below) has the highest island population at 120 million – that is about 1,000 people for every square kilometre. Indonesia is made up of more than 13,000 islands.

4. The smallest island that is a country is Nauru, in the Pacific Ocean. The whole island is only 20 km².

5. Manitoulin Island in Lake Huron, Canada, is the largest island in a lake.

6. The world's most remote island with people living on it is Tristan da Cunha. It is about 2,800 kilometres west of South Africa and about the same distance east of South America.

7. One of the newest islands is part of Tonga in the Pacific Ocean. The island was formed when an undersea volcano erupted in June 1995.

8. Tebua Tarawa and Abanuea, two South Pacific islands in Kiribati, disappeared in 1999 as sea levels rose to new heights.

9 The island country most at risk from sea level rise is the Maldives in the Indian Ocean. The highest point is just over 2 metres above sea level.

10 Lakshadweep Islands, off south-west India, means 100,000 islands when translated. There are only 27!

The World's Major Island Groups

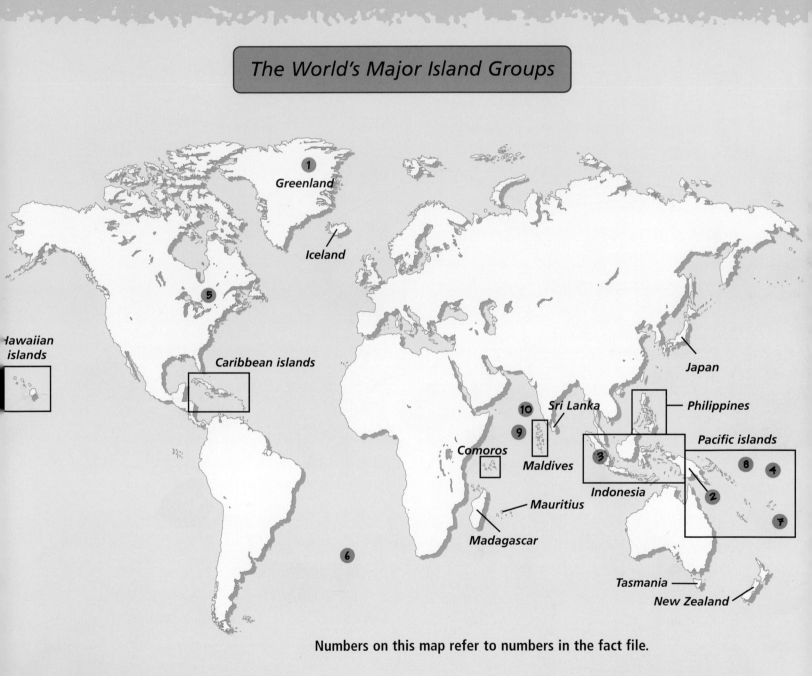

1 Greenland

Iceland

5

Hawaiian islands

Caribbean islands

Japan

10 Sri Lanka

9

Philippines

Comoros

Maldives

Pacific islands

3

8 **4**

Indonesia

2

7

Mauritius

Madagascar

6

Tasmania

New Zealand

Numbers on this map refer to numbers in the fact file.

Glossary

Adapt Change in some way.

Arc A curved line.

Archipelago A group of islands.

Arctic The area around the North Pole.

Atoll A ring-shaped island made from a coral reef, surrounding a volcanic island.

Causeway A road that is covered by the sea at high tide.

Climate The normal weather for an area of the world.

Coast The place where land meets the sea.

Continent A continuous area of land, usually containing several countries.

Coral A hard, rock-like substance built up by animals in warm seas.

Coral reef A bank of coral, where lots of tropical fish swim.

Currents Strong, underwater movements of the sea.

Desert An area of land with a dry climate. It can be sandy or rocky.

Environment The natural surroundings of an area.

Equator An imaginary line around the middle of the Earth.

Erode Wear away the land.

Erupt When magma, gases and ash are forced through the surface of the Earth.

Fresh water Drinking water. Sea water contains salt and cannot be drunk by humans.

Isolated Cut-off from anywhere else.

Lagoon A saltwater lake or shallow sea surrounded by a coral island.

Lava Molten rocks that erupt from volcanoes.

Magma Hot, liquid rock that is found under the Earth's surface.

Mainland The main area of a continent or a country, not the islands around it.

North Pole The point on the globe that is furthest north.

Port A place where ships load and unload the goods that they carry.

Predator An animal that hunts other animals.

Remote Far away.

Sandbank A bank of sand underwater or above sea level.

South Pole The point on the globe that is furthest south.

Tide The rising and falling of the sea.

Uninhabited A place without people living there.

Volcano A place where lava, ash and gases erupt from beneath the Earth's surface.

Further information

Books to Read:

Bustling Coastlines (The Natural World) by Barbara Taylor (Ticktock Media, 2000)

Coasts (Earth in Danger) by Polly Goodman (Hodder Wayland, 2001)

Coasts (Geography First) by Kay Barnham (Hodder Wayland, 2004)

Islands and Seasides (Curriculum Focus) by David Flint (Hopscotch Educational Publishing, 2003)

Seashore (DK Eyewitness Guides) by Steve Parker (Dorling Kindersley, 1989)

Volcanoes (Geography First) by Christopher Durbin (Hodder Wayland, 2004)

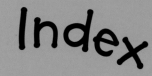

Index

All the numbers in **bold** refer to photographs and illustrations as well as text.